Easy R Programming for Beginners

Your Step-By-Step Guide to Learning R Programming

Felix Alvaro

Table of Contents

Acknowledgments

Firstly, I want to thank God for giving me the knowledge and inspiration to put this informative book together. I also want to thank my parents, my brothers and my partner Silvia for their support.

Introduction

Hello there! Three Cheers for investing in this Guide!

You have certainly taken a vital step towards learning R Programming language. What you are going to learn in this step-by-step beginner's guide, is how to master the fundamentals of such a gorgeous open-source programming language, which includes vectors, data frames and lists.

With more than two million global users, R language is rapidly turning into a top programming language specifically in the space of data science, as well as statistics. The figures of R language users have grown by forty percent each year, and an increasing number of organizations are utilizing this language in their everyday activities.

Now, for some individuals, R language can initially be quite intimidating. For the simple reason that it's way more complex than other languages, because the syntax of R Programming is different from those of several other programming languages. Numerous professional programming language writers have found R as challenging! According to them, R is really pretty simple, except it is unconventional. With the help of this guide you'll not only gain all the vital knowledge about learning R language efficiently, you'll also be geared up to carry out your own initial data-analysis.

My name is Felix Alvaro, and I am a passionate and experienced Web Designer & Programmer, Mentor, Entrepreneur, and Author. My mission is to inspire and motivate you to attain all your future objectives, by sharing my experience and knowledge through my books.

Regardless of whether or not you're proficient in any other programming language, even if you're just a beginner, you have certainly opted for the right guide to learn R language. I can assure you that this step-by-step guide will immensely assist you in mastering the fundamentals of R language, which is open-source, free, potent and greatly extendable.

Once you go through this entire book, you'll come to know how easy it was to learn R! In this guide, I have unfolded layer-by-layer, the secrecy surrounding R Programming, so that you can effortlessly grasp everything fairly quickly.

So, without further ado, LET'S GET STARTED!

In the first chapter, we'll discuss a brief history of R Programming, what exactly R Programming is, and the benefits of using R language.

Chapter One: An Introduction to R Programming

With more than two million global users, R language is rapidly turning into a top programming language specifically in the space of data science, as well as statistics. And, since its inception as an 'Academic-Demonstration-Language' during the 1990s, the R language has swiftly developed and extended. The figures of R language users have grown by forty percent each year, and an increasing number of organizations are utilizing this language in their everyday activities.

A Brief History of R:

The R language was created and developed by two colleagues at the 'University of Auckland, New Zealand', during the 1990s - **Ross Ihaka and Robert Gentleman**. They created R as a free software environment for the purpose of educating their students. And, as they both were pretty acquainted with the S language (S is a commercial programming language for statistics), they decided to utilize the similar syntax, and hence, created R. Ross Ihaka and Robert Gentleman then publicized their new software on the 'S-news Mailing List'. Many individuals started paying attention, and began to team up with them, particularly Martin Machler.

At present, only a group of eighteen individuals, also known as the 'R Development Core Team', possess the exclusive rights to alter the source code's central archive. Additionally, various other individuals have significantly contributed to the development of R.

Below are the significant milestone years in relation to the development of R:

- **During the 1990s:** R was created, and its development began.
- **In 1993:** R Programming was announced for the first time on 'S-news Mailing List'. And, since its inception, a bunch of active R mailing-lists has been formed. You can log on to https://www.r-project.org/mail.html and get access to descriptions of these lists as well as all the subscription instructions.
- **In 1995:** Martin Machler persuaded the entire group to make the R language code as **Free Software**. After that, the R language code was licensed under the 'Free Software Foundation's GNU General Public License'.
- **In 1997:** The first R Development Core Team was established.
- **In early 2000:** The initial version of R language (version 1.0.0) was released.

What exactly is R Programming?

R is a programming language which is used by many scientists, data analysts and numerous statisticians, to analyse databases, and to carry out statistical scrutiny with figures, as well as graphs.

R language is an awesome tool to analyse huge data volumes. If your job involves huge data analysis (huge database and files), then you can utilize R to fetch your data and perform certain processing tasks on it. R comes with various supplementary packages which you can download, and which will even allow you to simplify or expand various commands, while you analyse your data.

What are the benefits of using R language?

Following are some of the prominent benefits of using R:

R is an open-source code, and it is free:

Anyone can get access to R under an open-source license. It means that you are allowed to download, as well as alter, the code. It is even available free of cost. These are the biggest benefits of R - you can download as well as utilize R for free! An additional benefit is, any individual has the right to utilize the source code, alter it, and even develop it. Consequently, several exceptional programmers have significantly contributed enhancements, and modernized the R code. And that's the reason why R is so stable, secure and dependable.

R can run anywhere:

The 'R-Development-Core-Team' has made a lot of efforts, and put a lot of emphasis into making R compatible with diverse forms of software, as well as hardware. As a result, R is now available for Mac, Windows, and UNIX systems.

R is extensible:

R is a powerful language which performs numerous functions. For instance, graphics, statistical analysis, and manipulation of huge databases. However, one huge benefit of R is that it's greatly extensible. Various programmers can effortlessly write down their software, and then distribute them as add-on-packages. And due to this effortlessness of crafting such add-on-packages, factually thousands of such packages exist. In reality, numerous new statistical analysis techniques are regularly made available, which are attached with an R package.

R offers an engaged group:

The user base of R is rapidly emerging. Numerous individuals who utilize R, in due course, initiate to assist new users, as well as promote the use of R in their certified circles and at their place of work. Occasionally, they also tend to get active on the R mailing-lists, or Q&A (question & answer) websites, for instance 'Stack-Overflow'. Other than such mailing lists, and question & answer websites, they even join various social networks, for instance, Twitter, Facebook, and various provincial R user forums.

R effectively links with various other programming languages:

With growing number of individuals moving towards R for their data-analysis, they began to make attempts to merge R with their existing workflows. This led to an entire array of packages for the purpose of connecting R to various databases, file-systems, and numerous other applications. Several such packages have been effectively linked to R ever since. For instance, the 'R-package-foreign' is a division of the 'Standard-R-distribution', and it allows you to interpret data from the 'Statistical-Packages' such as SAS, SPSS, STATA, and various others. Numerous add-on packages are there in order to link R to various database systems. For instance, the 'RODBC package' to interpret data utilizing the ODBC (Open Database Connectivity protocol), and the 'ROracle package' to interpret 'Oracle databases'.

R processes more than Statistics only:

R was created and developed initially by statisticians in order to simplify the entire statistical procedure. And, this legacy is still moving forward, which has turned R into a very potent tool to perform practically any statistical calculation. Since R began to develop away from its genesis in statistics, numerous individuals who usually think of themselves as software-programmers instead of statisticians, have grown to get engaged with R. And consequently, R has now become highly useful for an extensive range of non-statistical assignments, which comprises graphic visualization, data processing as well as all sorts of data scrutiny. R is effectively being utilized in the various areas of genetics, finance, natural language processing, market research, biology, and many more.

In this chapter, we've discussed a brief history of R Programming, what exactly R programming is, and what are the benefits of using R language.

****

In the next chapter, we'll discuss how to install R and R Studio, the right code editors to begin coding R Programming, working with your code editors, the initial R session, how to source a script, and ways to navigate the workspace.

13

Chapter Two: How to Get Started

In this chapter, we'll discuss how to install R and R Studio, the right code editors to begin coding R Programming, working with your code editors, the initial R session, how to source a script, and ways to navigate the workspace.

How to install R and R Studio

Prior to using R, you have to install R, to begin with. And, even though you can utilize the in-built code editor, you might also wish to install an editor with advanced functions. As R Studio runs on every platform and is incorporated smoothly with R, we'll also talk about the R Studio installation.

Installing R:

It's not that complicated to install R; however, fine-tuning it to make it compatible to your requirements necessitates a little tweaking. You can locate all the essential installation files, and all required details about the installation process at CRAN (Comprehensive R Archive Network) site. Pick the link for your preferred OS (Operating System) that will further advance you to the download site to obtain the newest R distribution. To get all the comprehensive installation information, just log on to (https://cran.r-project.org/doc/manuals/R-admin.html).

Following are the installation steps for Windows users:

- Visit CRAN (CRAN; https://cran.r-project.org/).
- Click '**Download R for Windows**' option.

The Comprehensive R Archive Network

Download and Install R

Precompiled binary distributions of the base system and contributed packages,
Windows and Mac users most likely want one of these versions of R:

- Download R for Linux
- Download R for (Mac) OS X
- Download R for Windows ← **CLICK HERE**

R is part of many Linux distributions, you should check with your Linux package
management system in addition to the link above.

- After that click '**Base**' option, and get (download)
  the '**Installer File**' for the newest version of R.

R for Windows

Subdirectories: **Click Here**

base   Binaries for base distribution (managed by Duncan Murdoch). This is what you
                want to **install R for the first time**.

contrib   Binaries of contributed CRAN packages (for R >= 2.11.x; managed by Uwe
                Ligges). There is also information on third party software available for CRAN
                Windows services and corresponding environment and make variables.

old contrib   Binaries of contributed CRAN packages for outdated versions of R (for R <
                2.11.x; managed by Uwe Ligges).

Rtools   Tools to build R and R packages (managed by Duncan Murdoch). This is what
                you want to build your own packages on Windows, or to build R itself.

- Then right click on the '**Installer File**' and choose 'Run-as-Administrator' option.

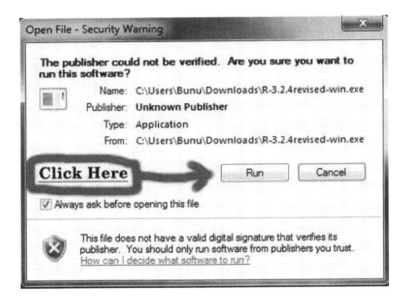

- Pick the language you prefer, which will be used all through the installation process. Now, this step won't alter the R language, and the entire Help file as well as messages will continue in English.
- Carefully follow all the instructions. You can even opt for all the default settings, which are safe and secure, and keep on clicking 'Next' button, till R begins to install.

R is available for both 64- bit and 32- bit Windows version. In case you own a 64-bit Windows OS, you can simply install both the versions. The 'Installer File' will also perform this task. And, for any other versions, you can certainly get further details at the R Installation site mentioned above. The R version for 32-bit is entirely brilliant, and occasionally this version is a little faster as compared to the R version for 64- bit system. You might require the 64- bit R version just in case you need that extra memory.

For Linux & Mac Users:

For those who own Linux and Mac OS, they're specifically advised to carefully read the entire instructions and information, when they log on to the 'CRAN' site. R can be easily installed and run on every single system. However, on the basis of your version of Linux or Mac, you might be required to follow specific instructions to efficiently install R. And, if you don't follow those instructions carefully, it might cause harm to your system.

Installing R Studio:

R Studio version is a quite new and relatively polished editor for R. Usually, it is highly recommended as it is pretty simple to use. It has great support system, comes with a decent 'Help-page', and integrates R in a realistic manner.

Following are the simple steps to install R Studio:

- Log on to (
  https://www.rstudio.com/products/rstudio2/.)
- Then click the '**RStudio Desktop**' button.

- Pick the 'Installer file' in accordance with your system versions.
- Next, click the 'Run' option.

Subsequently, R Studio will get installed on your particular system. R Studio by default will detect your newly installed R version, and you can utilize R from inside R Studio. Plus, you won't be requiring any additional configuration.

What are the right code editors to begin coding R Programming?

To begin coding in R, you'll require an editing tool. Now, whichever editing tool that you utilize will depend on your OS (Operating System) in some measure, as R itself doesn't offer any particular graphical editor for any OS (Operating System).

The primary R install provides you the following:

- **For Windows version:** An editor known as 'R Gui'.
- **For Mac OS X version:** An editor known as 'R.app'.
- **For Linux version:** There isn't any precise editor for Linux version; however, you can utilize other editors such as 'Emacs' or 'Vim'.

Realistically, such dissimilarities among the various OS (Operating Systems) hardly matter, as R is fundamentally a programming language, and can efficiently understand your code equally across all these different OS.

Other R editor options:

R provides you with the full liberty to pick your own code editor, and development settings. It's not at all mandatory for you to use only the typical R editors, or R Studio.

Following are a few alternatives which you can consider:

- **ESS (Emacs Speaks Statistics):** Emacs is a great text as well as code editor, and is extensively utilized in the Linux systems worldwide. It's even available for Windows versions. ESS has a global fan-base, and is quite renowned for its keyboard-shortcuts for nearly everything one can possibly do. So, in case you're a Linux programmer, Emacs editor possibly could be a fine option for you. Visit (http://ess.r-project.org/) for further information.
- **Eclipse StatET:** Is one more greatly incorporated development setting, and comes with an 'R add-in' known as 'StatET'. So, in case you have already finished software-development on huge assignments, then Eclipse could be a fine option for you. You're required to install Java on your system. Visit (http://www.walware.de/goto/statet).
- **Tinn-R:** Tinn-R was created and developed particularly to work with R, and is currently available just for Windows version. Tinn-R has certain good features which will enable you to set-up R scripts collections in assignments. It is quite simple to install and utilize, as compared to Emacs

and Eclipse editors; however, it certainly lacks a lot of features comparatively. Visit (http://www.sciviews.org/Tinn-R).

How to work with your code editors?

R is a programming language, and not an application. It literally means that the users have the full liberty to pick their own editing tools to perform coding in R. Now, we'll talk about the R editor for the Windows version called R Graphical User Interface (R Gui).

R Gui:

When you download and install R, along with the entire process, you acquire the standard R Gui (R Graphical User Interface) by default. R Gui provides you with certain tools to handle your R settings, primarily your R console window. On this console window, you have to type scripts or instructions, and command R to perform helpful tasks.

Viewing your R console:

After the successful installation of R in your system, shortcuts will be created in your Windows Startup menu. In your Windows Startup menu, search for the R folder and then look for an R icon followed by a version series.

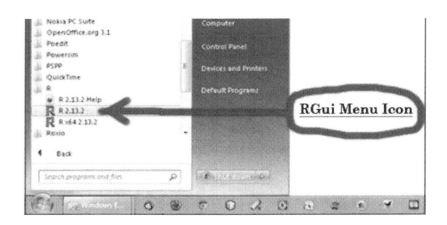

When you click on the RGui icon, you'll view for the first time, the R Console screen with a few basic details like the R version and the licensing statements. At the lowest end of all these basic details is the '**R prompt**', represented by a '>' mark. This R prompt sign point towards where you're supposed to type your commands. You'll even notice a blinking pointer at the prompt's right side.

R console for 'Windows' Version:

22

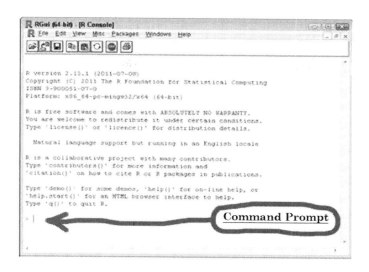

R Console for 'Mac' Version:

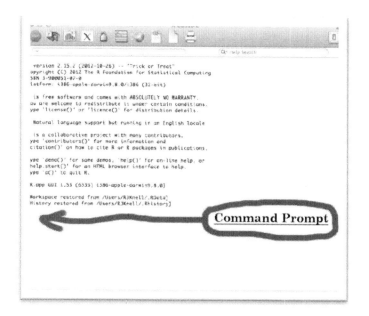

As you can make out from the above two figures, the R console is same for both the Windows and Mac version.

How to close the R console?

In order to close your R console, you need to type the following just after the (>) sign (R command prompt sign):

> q( )

R will ask you to ensure that you really want to quit.

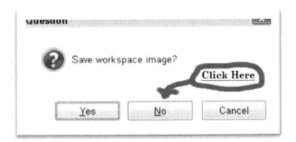

Just Click on 'No' option, as you have nothing to save yet. Your R session will close.

R Studio editor:

To work in R Studio editor, first of all, click on the R Studio icon in your Windows Start-up menu.

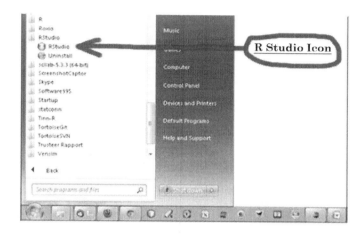

After that, Select File>New>R Script. You'll see 4 work areas:

- **Source Editor:** Source is a text-editor which enables you to work with 'Source-Script-Files'. You can type here several rows of code, save the script-file to hard disk, and carry out various vital tasks. Source editor functions are similar to any other text editor you've worked with; however, it's quite intelligent. It identifies as well as emphasizes on numerous constituents of your code, for instance, diverse colors for unrelated elements.
- **Console:** The console area in R Studio is quite similar to the RGui console. This is where you have to type scripts or instructions, and command R to perform helpful tasks.
- **Workspace/History:** In the workspace/history area you can examine the variables you formed during your R session, along with their values. In this area, you can also view all the commands history, which you typed in R.

- **Files/packages/plots/help:** In this area, you can gain access to various helpful tools.

    - **Files:** Here you can look through all the files and related folders on your system.
    - **Packages:** Here you can see all the installed-packages lists. A package is autonomous code set which enhances the performance of R.
    - **Plots:** Here R exhibits your plots, such as graphs or charts.
    - **Help:** Here you can look through the in-built 'Help-system' of R.

Your initial R session:

A majority of programming books usually begin with an easy program. Typically, this initial program is to generate a message called 'Welcome Sir!' Here is how we do it.

Initiate a new R session and then type the below mentioned command in your R console:

> **print("Welcome Sir!")**

Press Enter. R instantly responds with the following:

[1] "Welcome Sir!"

Well done! You've just finished your initial R script!

Next, we'll check how to perform a simple calculation successfully. The following are just a few simple codes of commands. We'll discuss all these in details in the coming chapters:

Performing simple calculations:

Type the below mentioned command in your console to compute the sum of 5 digits:

> 1+2+3+4+5

[1] 15

The result is 15.

Vectors:

A vector is a basic data-structure form. As per definition, a vector is a single unit which consists of a set of things. For instance, a set of digits is a numeric vector.

To create a vector, just type the below mentioned command in your console:

```
> c(1,2,3,4,5)
[1] 1 2 3 4 5
```

Here, you've not only just created a vector; you also have effectively utilized a function in R.

Function:

A function is a section of code which intakes certain inputs, and performs something unique with those values. While creating a vector above, you command the c( ) function to create a vector with the initial 5 integers. The values inside the brackets are known as 'arguments'. You can even create a vector by utilizing operators. Now, an operator is a sign you insert between two entries to perform any math calculation. The signs (+, -, *, /) are called operators. Another useful operator is known as sequence, and it appears similar to a colon sign (:).

Type the below mentioned command in your console:

> 1:5

[1] 1 2 3 4 5

Well done! You've again created a vector! Type the below mentioned command in your console to compute the sum of above vector:

> sum(1:5)

[1] 15

How to store and calculate values

The symbol (<-) is the assignment operator here. You need to type less than sign (<), and a hyphen symbol (-) after it. Type the below mentioned command in your console:

> a <- 1:5

```
> a
```

`[1] 1 2 3 4 5`

Here, you initially assigned the 1:5 (sequence) to a (variable). After that, you typed 'a' in the console, and then pressed 'Enter' key to get the final result.

You can even perform calculations on those values. Construct another variable b, and assign it some value, for instance 20. After that, add the values of both the variables (a & b):

```
> b <- 20
> a + b
```

`[1] 21 22 23 24 25`

Now construct a new variable, and name it c. Then assign c the value (a + b):

```
> c <- a + b
> c
```

`[1] 21 22 23 24 25`

Here, one important thing which you can notice is that the values of both the variables didn't change at all. And, it won't change until a new value is assigned to them.

You can even assign text value to a variable. Create a variable x, and assign it Welcome text by putting it inside " ":

> x <- "Welcome"

> x

[1] "Welcome"

You can even utilize the c( ) function to combine text. Create a variable n and assign it the value of c( ):

> n <- c("Welcome", "Sir!")

> n

[1] "Welcome" "Sir!"

You can utilize the **paste( )** function to link together multiple texts. The **paste( )** function automatically places a space in-between different texts:

> paste("Welcome", "Sir!")

[1] "Welcome Sir!"

These were some of the basic calculations which you can do in R. Now, we'll talk about various other things which we can perform in R.

How to source a script

Now, it's time to move a level up, and command R to carry out various commands one after another, with no need to wait for further instructions. In R, the source( ) function is utilized to run a whole script, and its users call this entire procedure as 'Sourcing-a-Script'.

In order to set up your script which is to be sourced, you're required to first type your whole script in your editor. Here, we are using the R Studio editor. Just type the below mentioned code in the R Studio editor:

>b <- "Hey!"

>n <- readline("What is my name?")

```
>print(paste(b, n))
```

You can enter numerous lines of code in your R Studio
editor. After that, when everything is set-up, you can source the
script (send the commands to R). In case of R Studio or RGui,
you can perform this task by any one of the following methods:

- **Transfer a single line of code from your source
  editor to your console:** Just click on the single line
  of code that you wish to run, and after that press
  '**Ctrl+R**' keys in RGui editor. You need to press
  '**Ctrl+Enter**' keys, or click on the '**Run**' button in R
  Studio editor.
- **Transfer a chunk of desired code to your console:**
  First, select the entire chunk of desired code that you
  wish to run, and after that press '**Ctrl+Enter**' keys
  in R Studio, or press '**Ctrl+R**' keys in RGui editor.
- **Source a script, or transfer the whole script to
  your console:** In case of R Studio, just click on the
  source editor section and then press '**Ctrl + Shift +
  Enter**' keys, or click on the '**Source'** button. In case
  of RGui, just click on your script window, and then
  select '**Edit>Run all**'.

You can now transfer your whole script to your R console.
Just click on the '**Source**' button in the source editor section, or
select '**Edit>Source**'. Your above- mentioned script will begin,
and reach the end where it will ask to enter some values, and then

will wait for you to type your name in your console window
section.

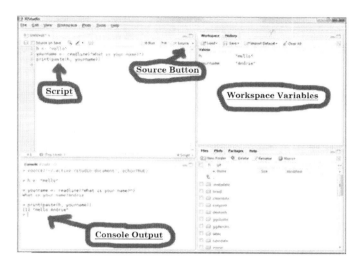

Ways to navigate the workspace:

The workspace means the collection of all the functions as
well as variables, which you have built all through the session,
along with any of the packages which are loaded. Time and again,
you will wish to remind yourself about all the variables which
you've saved in the workspace. You can utilize the ls( ) function
to get the list of all the objects (functions, variables etc.) in the
workspace. Just type ls( ) in your R console:

```
> ls( )
```

[1] "a" "go" "k" "l" "normal" "m"

R will notify you of all the names of every single variable which you have created.

Ways to manipulate the workspace contents:

In case you feel like you don't require some of the workspace objects, you can easily get rid of them. For instance, you don't require object m anymore, and you want to remove it from your workspace. Now to get rid of it, just utilize the **rm( )** function, and after that again utilize the **ls( )** function to crosscheck your workspace contents:

```
> rm(m)
> ls( )
```

[1] "a" "go" "k" "l" "normal"

You can see that the object m doesn't exist anymore.

Ways to save your work:

There are various options to save your work:

- The **save( )** function to secure your individual variables.
- The **save.image( )** function to save your whole workspace.
- You can save your R script file, using the appropriate save menu command in your code editor.

For instance, if you wish to save the value of **"normal"** variable. Just perform the following:

- Search for the working directory where R will save your file. You need to type the following command:
  > **>getwd()**
  > **[1] "c:/users/delfim"**
  >
  > Typically, your user folder is the working directory where your file is saved automatically. The precise name as well as the folder's path actually depends on your OS (Operating System).
- Type the below mentioned command in your R console using any name such as myname.rda, and after that press 'Enter' key:
  > **>save(normal, file= "myname.rda")**
  > R will save your file in the working directory. And, in case the process is

successfully over, then you won't receive any affirmation message.

- And, to ensure that the entire process was successfully over, you can crosscheck your folder browser to verify, whether or not, the new file exists.

*****

In this chapter, we have discussed how to install R and R Studio, the right code editors to begin coding R Programming, working with your code editors, the initial R session, how to source a script, and ways to navigate the workspace.

In the next chapter, we'll talk about the basics of R programming

Chapter Three: The Basics of R Programming

In this chapter, we will discuss the fundamentals of R Syntax, how to effectively use function & arguments, how to make your code plain & readable, and how to broaden R programming with user packages.

The Fundamentals of R Syntax (How to write the right R code):

In this section, we'll focus on certain precise tasks in order to write the right R code, and discuss how these are to be done in R.

Expressions:

An expression means a specific command to carry out a specific task. For instance, the following expression commands R to add the first five integers together:

```
> 1+2+3+4+5
[1] 15
```

The result is 15.

In a case in which there exists numerous expressions, then they are run in a sequence (in the order these emerge) one-at-a-time. The following few sections will illustrate some of the fundamental R expressions types.

Constant values expressions:

These are the plainest type of R expression. Constant value is usually a number (numeric value), or a character text. For instance, if we have to state the number of seconds in 5 minutes, we denote a number.

> 300

[1] 300

In a case in which we have to state the filename which we wish to interpret data from, we denote the filename as a character text values. The character text values ought to be enclosed by either double quotes (" "), or single quotes (' ').

>"How are you?"

[1] "How are you?"

Arithmetic expressions:

An arithmetic expression is somewhat more of a composite expression, and is used for calculating with numeric values. R comes with certain standard arithmetic operators:

+ (Symbol for addition)

- (Symbol for subtraction)

* (Symbol for multiplication)

/ (Symbol for division)

^ (Symbol for exponentiation)

The brackets (parentheses) are used to manage the order of calculation. R follows the usual BODMAS system of primacy regarding all the arithmetic operators; however, brackets (parentheses) are a handy means to avoid any mistakes. Following is an example:

>(78963-56397)/10

[1] 2256.6

Conditions expressions:

A condition expression means, either a yes or no, as an answer. The outcome of a condition expression is a logical value (either true or false). R comes with certain standard operators to compare different values, along with certain operators to combine those conditions:

$==$ **(symbol for equality)**

>and>= (symbol for greater than or equal to)

<and<= (symbol for less than or equal to)

!=   **(symbol for inequality)**

&&   **(symbol for logical and)**

ǁ   **(symbol for logical or)**

!   **(Symbol for logical not)**

Following is an example where the code enquires, whether or not, the 2nd population assessment outsize the 1st population, and the 2nd population assessment is greater than 1 billion.

>(population2 > population1) && (population2 > 1,000,000,000)

42

[1] TRUE

Function calls:

One of the most helpful R expressions is called function call. These are quite significant as they will enable you to utilize R to carry out any key task. A function call is fundamentally a composite command, and there exists hundreds and thousands of such functions which carry out diverse tasks. We'll discuss certain key functions to manipulate data in later chapters.

A function call comprises the name of the function followed by arguments (within brackets) which provide essential details for the function to carry out the task. The arguments are separated by commas. Following is an example:

c( ) function to combine text:

> c("Welcome", "Sir!")

And when you press 'ENTER' key the result is:

[1] "Welcome" "Sir!"

Symbols:

Everything we type in console which begins with a letter, and is not any of the specific R keywords, is read by R as a symbol. A symbol means a tag for an entity which is presently saved in RAM. Now, when R comes across any symbol, it pulls out from RAM the value corresponding to that tag.

R by default comes with certain pre-defined values along with certain related symbols. For instance, there is a pre-defined symbol **pi**.

>pi

[1] 3.141593

Keywords:

There are certain symbols or keywords which are only used to symbolize unique values and these can't be re-assigned:

- **NA** is a keyword which symbolizes a lost or unidentified value.
- **Inf** is a keyword which symbolizes infinity.
- **NaN** is a keyword which symbolizes an arithmetic outcome which is not defined.
- **NULL** is a keyword which symbolizes an empty outcome. Certain R functions might not generate any outcome, and the result is NULL.
- **TRUE & FALSE** are the keywords which symbolizes the logical values "true" and "false".

Ways to name variables:

While writing code, as we frequently assign values to various symbols, we are compelled to invent a great deal of diverse variable names. It is vital to pick rational variable names for the following reasons:

- A fine name is a sort of credential. A name such as "PlaceOfBirth" tells the reader a lot of things about the kind of value which has been assigned to that particular variable, as compared to names such as p, or pob.
- Short or handy names like a, or aa, or aaa, must be avoided as it will simply create a lot of errors when you unknowingly reuse the similar short name for diverse tasks.

- You should make use of a combination of upper and lower- case letters. You should create the name just like a small sentence, and begin every new word with a capital letter such as "PlaceOfBirth" .

These were some of the fundamentals of R syntax. Now, we'll discuss the effective use of functions and arguments.

How to effectively use function & arguments

Ways to vectorize the functions:

The process involves creation of vectors, and placing them inside the function. Vectorizing the functions are quite an effective function of R; however, various professionals who are not very experienced with R, frequently face difficulties in the beginning, as they are not aware of such concept. Any function which is vectorized, affects not only a solo value, but also the entire vector values simultaneously. Vectorizing the functions in R will certainly simplify the code.

First and foremost, you need to create a vector. You can utilize the c( ) function, and the values need to be separated by commas (,). Following is an example:

Just assume that Phillip is playing basketball with his friends, and his brother is keeping a tally of the Phillip's baskets in every game. After five games, Phillip asks his brother about how many baskets he had made so far. Now, the number of baskets made by him can be put in a vector in the following way:

> **> Phillip <- c(10,5,5,4,8)**

> **> Phillip**

> **[1] 10 5 5 4 8**

And, to know the total number of baskets made by Phillip, you can use the **sum ( )** function:

> **> sum (Phillip)**

> **[1] 32**

Another example is the **paste ( )** function. In case you create a vector with just the names of various fruits, **paste ( )** can add the text "fruit" next to all of them with a single command. Here is the example:

> **> Fruitnames <- c("Apple", "Banana", "Orange")**

```
> addname <- "Fruit"

> paste(Fruitnames, addname)

[1] "Apple Fruit" "Banana Fruit" "Orange Fruit"
```

R can even mix two long vectors element-wise. Following is the example:

```
> Fighters <- c("Fedor", "Jon")

> last.names <- c("Emilianenko", "Jones")

> paste(Fighters, last.names)

[1] "Fedor Emilianenko" "Jon Jones"
```

You just don't need to write any complex code. You just have to create vectors, and place them inside the function. Now, we'll discuss the ways to place arguments in a function.

Ways to place argument within a function:

Arguments provide specific details about precisely what a function is meant to execute. You can use 2 general arguments types in R:

- Arguments having default values.
- Arguments devoid of default values.

In case an argument is devoid of any default value, then the value might be compulsory or optional. Usually, the first argument is always necessary. Type and execute the following code in your console:

> **print( )**

R will inform you that the command requires the argument 'x':

(Error in .Internal(print.default(x, digits, quote, na.print, print.gap, : 'x' is missing)

Now, you need to assign an argument in the following way:

> **print(x = "What is my name?")**

Or

```
> print("What is my name?")
```

These were some examples of how to place argument in your function. Now we'll discuss the ways to make your code plain & readable.

How to make your code plain & readable

When you initially begin using functions to carry out complicated calculations, your entire code might become a huge mess of symbols as well as texts. Fortunately, we are here to tell you certain tips & tricks, to clean-up your code, and to make it more readable.

Using functions and performing difficult calculations could result in longer lines of code in R. R allows you break up your line of code into multiple lines, just like any normal text editor, in your entire script. And, you also don't need to utilize any specific character to achieve this. R will interpret that the line of code isn't over yet, provided that you offer it certain clues. You need to ensure that your command is definitely unfinished. Following are the techniques to do this:

- **Utilize a quotation-mark to begin a string:** R would consider the entire input which will follow the 1st quotation-mark, even the line-breaks, as an element of the string, till it encounters the 2nd quotation-mark.

- **End the unfinished command with an operator symbol (such as +, /, <- etc.):** R would interpret that some more code is to follow, and will allow you to build structure in huge and complex calculations.
- **Open a bracket (parenthesis) for a function:** R would interpret the entire input it receives as a single line, till it encounters the 2nd matching bracket (parenthesis).

Next, we'll discuss the ways to broaden R programming with user packages.

How to broaden R Programming with user packages?

The actual power of R is that it allows everybody to write their own functions as well as share those functions with other numerous R users in a structured way. Several programmers have written suitable functions in R, and quite frequently a fresh statistical technique gets published every now and then. Many such programmers then share their code which is known as R package. These user packages are the compilations of R code, data-sets, Help-files etc., and can be simply integrated into R.

Ways to find R packages:

Numerous websites (also known as repositories) provide various R packages. The most renowned website is CRAN (Comprehensive R Archive Network) where you can easily access several user packages. Visit (https://cran.r-project.org/doc/manuals/R-admin.html)

CRAN also possesses a set of file-packages as well as the reference manuals. CRAN even allows the users to verify whether or not a user-package is still preserved, and to get an outline of the modifications done in the package.

Ways to install R packages:

In order to install an R package you need to use with the function called **install.packages( )**. For instance, if you wish to install the 'lubridate' package, you just need to write the package's name (here it's 'lubridate') as a string in the **install.packages( )** function.

The 'lubridate' package contains various significant tools which allow the users to easily work with dates as well as times. Following is the way to install the user package:

> **install.packages('lubridate')**

Ways to load and unload user packages:

Prior to using any user-package, you need to load it into R first of all, and for that you need to utilize the **library( )** function. Following is the command to load any user package:

> **library(lubridate)**

And, in case you wish to unload any user-package, then you'll need to utilize the **detach( )** function. However, you need to specifically denote that it's a user-package which you wish to unload. Following is the command to unload any user package:

> **detach(package:lubridate)**

These were some of the important ways to broaden R programming with user packages.

****

In this chapter, we discussed the fundamentals of R Syntax, how to effectively use function & arguments, how to make your code plain & readable, and how to broaden R Programming with user packages.

In the next chapter, we'll talk about the ways of getting started working in R.

Chapter Four: Getting started, working in R

In this chapter, we'll discuss the various ways of getting started working in R. We'll cover diverse topics such as fundamentals of arithmetic, how to organize data in Vectors, how to work with logical vectors, manipulating text, vector & matrix, data frames, and creation of lists.

Fundamentals of Arithmetic (working with numbers, lost values, & infinity):

R comes with 4 diverse groups of statistical functions as well as operators:

- **Essential arithmetic operators:** Such operators are being utilized in nearly all the programming languages.
- **Mathematical functions:** You can get such advanced functions on any calculator.
- **Vector operations:** These are functions which do calculations on an entire vector, such as **sum( )**. The outcome depends on different values of the vector.
- **Matrix operations:** Such functions are utilized for calculations as well as various operations. We'll talk about matrix operations later in the chapter.

First, we'll discuss the arithmetic operators, mathematical functions, and vector operations.

Ways to use the arithmetic operators:

Below is the table of some of the fundamental arithmetic operators.

Operator	Description	Example
x + y	y added to x	2 + 3 = 5
x − y	y subtracted from x	8 − 2 = 6
x * y	x multiplied by y	3 * 2 = 6
x / y	x divided by y	10 / 5 = 2
x ^ y (or x ** y)	x raised to the power y	2 ^ 5 = 32
x %% y	remainder of x divided by y (x mod y)	7 %% 3 = 1
x %/% y	x divided by y but rounded down (integer divide)	7 %/% 3 = 2

All the operators in the above- mentioned table are vectorized operators. By utilizing them, you'll be able to perform difficult calculations with smaller code. Just consider the following example:

One vector symbolizes the count of baskets made by Phillip during the five basketball games, and the other vector symbolizes the count of baskets his buddy George made:

> Phillip.baskets <- c(10,3,3,5,8)

> George.baskets <- c(4,2,1,1,10)

Assume that their parents wish to pay them prize money for their efforts. Phillip gets 100 bucks per basket, and George gets 90 bucks per basket. Now, how to calculate the total collection?

The calculation is pretty simple in R. First of all, evaluate the cash each of them received per game:

> Phillip.money <- Phillip.baskets * 100

> George.money <- George.baskets * 90

Here, each of the vector value would be multiplied by the amount of cash. And, to obtain the total cash both of them received in each game, just type the following code:

> Phillip.money + George.money

[1] 1360 480 390 590 1700

You can even perform the calculation in a single line of code:

> **Phillip.baskets * 100 + George.baskets * 90**

[1] 1360 480 390 590 1700

Ways to use the mathematical functions:

R comes with an entire collection of functions which you can also find easily on any calculator. These are vectorized functions to help you perform complex calculations. Below is the table of some of the helpful mathematical functions:

Function	How it works?
abs(x)	Takes the absolute value of x
log(x,base=y)	Takes the logarithm of x with base y; if base is not specified, returns the natural logarithm
exp(x)	Returns the exponential of x
sqrt(x)	Returns the square root of x
factorial(x)	Returns the factorial of x (x!)
choose(x,y)	Returns the number of possible combinations when drawing y elements at a time from x possibilities

The potential of R goes way beyond this little table. We'll discuss certain specific calculations.

Ways to calculate logarithms as well as exponentials:

Type the following in the console to calculate the log from 1 to 3:

> log(1:3)

[1] 0.0000000 0.6931462 1.0976122

R will compute the natural logarithm in case the base value isn't stated. To compute the logarithm, for example, with base 6, type the following in the console:

> log(1:3,base=6)

[1] 0.0000000 0.3868427 0.6131471

Utilize **exp( )** function to perform the inverse of **log( )** function. The **exp( )** function elevates **y** to the power stated in the parenthesis:

```
> y <- log(1:3)

> exp(y)
```

Ways to use infinity function:

Sometimes, you simply don't possess the real values to compute with. In reality, in some data-sets a few values are lost and certain evaluations get infinity as an outcome, or can't be performed in any way. Fortunately, R is able to deal with all such circumstances.

In R, the following is the result when you attempt to divide any number by 0 (zero):

```
> 3/0
[1] Inf
```

Here, R appropriately informs you that the outcome is infinity. Also, negative-infinity is displayed as (- Inf).

```
> 5 – Inf
[1] –Inf
```

Now, to verify whether or not a number is infinite or finite, you need to utilize the functions **is.infinite()** and **is.finite()**. The **is.finite()** function will give a result **TRUE** in case the value is finite, and the **is.infinite()** will give a result **TRUE** in case the value is infinite.

Ways to deal with lost values:

One of the frequent issues with statistics computation is deficient data-sets. In order to deal with lost values, R utilizes a specific keyword called NA (which means Not Available). You're allowed to utilize NA as a suitable value, and you're even allowed to assign it as a value:

> y <- NA

However, bear in mind that calculations using an NA value will usually give NA as an outcome:

> y + 4

[1] NA

> log(y)

61

[1] NA

And, in case you wish to check whether or not a specific value is NA, you can utilize the function called **is.na()**:

> **is.na(y)**

[1] **TRUE**

Following is the table of results of functions infinite, NAN, and NA:

Functions	Results			
Function	Inf	−Inf	NaN	NA
is.finite()	FALSE	FALSE	FALSE	FALSE
is.infinite()	TRUE	TRUE	FALSE	FALSE
is.nan()	FALSE	FALSE	TRUE	FALSE
is.na()	FALSE	FALSE	TRUE	TRUE

These were some of the fundamentals of arithmetic. Now, we'll discuss the ways to organize data in Vectors.

How to organize data in vectors

In R, a vector is the smallest element with which you can perform your tasks. These possess both type as well as structure. Following are the vector types:

- **Numeric vectors:** It means all types of numeric values.
- **Integer vectors:** It means all integer values.
- **Logical vectors:** It means all logical values (TRUE or/and FALSE)
- **Character vectors:** It means all types of texts.
- **Date-time vectors:** It means dates as well as times in diverse formats.
- **Factors:** It means a unique vector type to work with certain groups.

Ways to create vectors:

In order to create a vector from a plain integer series, you can utilize the colon (:) operator. The code 4:9 will create a vector with the integers 4 to 9, and 5:-2 will create a vector with the integers 5 to –2.

And, in order to create larger or little steps in any sequence, you can utilize the **seq()** function. This special function lets you to state the quantity by which the figures should increase/decrease. Here's an example:

```
> seq(from = 5, to = 2, by = -1)
[1] 5 4 3 2
```

Ways to combine vectors:

The c( ) function represents concatenate in R. This function simply combines vectors. Consider the following example:

```
> Phillips.baskets <- c(10,3,3,5,8)
> George.baskets <- c(4,2,1,1,10)
> Total.baskets <-c(Phillips.baskets, George.baskets)
> Total.baskets
[1] 10 3 3 5 8 4 2 1 1 10
```

The outcome of this code represents a vector with all ten values. The c( ) function doesn't change the order of the digits. This implies that the vectors have an order. We'll discuss more about this order in the coming chapters.

Ways to repeat vectors:

R offers a specific function to repeat a vector which is known as **rep( )**. This function can be utilized in various ways. In case you wish to repeat the entire vector, you need to state the argument 'times'. In order to repeat the vector c(1,1, 6) four times, just type this command:

```
> rep(c(1,1,6), times = 4)

[1] 1 1 6 1 1 6 1 1 6 1 1 6
```

You can even repeat each of the value by stating the argument 'each':

```
> rep(c(1, 3,1), each = 4)

[1] 1 1 1 1 3 3 3 3 1 1 1 1
```

You can also inform R about the number of times each value needs to be repeated:

```
> rep(c(1, 6), times = c(3,4))

[1] 1 1 1 6 6 6 6
```

Now, utilize the argument 'l' to inform R about the length you desire. The vector will be repeated till it encounters your desired length, even in a case where the final repetition is unfinished. Consider the following example:

```
> rep(3:5,l=8)
[1] 3 4 5 3 4 5 3 4
```

These were some of the ways to organize data in a vector. Now, we'll discuss various ways to get values in and out of Vectors.

How to get values in and out of Vectors

You can carry out such tasks effortlessly by utilizing the advanced indexing system in R.

Knowing the indexing system:

Each time R displays a vector, it exhibits a numeric value like [1] ahead of any result. By displaying [1], R actually informs you about the location of the 1st position in the vector. It's actually the index position of that vector value. And, in case you create a lengthy vector, for instance from 1 to 20, then you'll view additional indices. Following is an example:

> n <- 20:1

> n

[1] 20 19 18 17 16 15 14 13 12 11 10 9 8 7 6 5 4

[18] 3 2 1 0

Here, R considers 3 as the 18th vector value. At the start of each line, R informs you about the index of the 1st value of that particular line.

Ways to extract values from any vector:

The brackets [ ] symbolize a powerful function in R which you can utilize to extract a value from any vector. Consider the above- mentioned example. You can acquire the 6th value of the **n** vector by typing the following:

> n[6]

[1] 15

The bracket [ ] function considers vectors like arguments. In a case in which you wish to pick beyond a single digit, then you can just mention a vector of indices like an argument within the [ ]:

> n[c(6,9,2)]

[1] 15 12 19

You can even save the indices, which you desire to extract, in a different vector and present that very vector like an argument:

> nd <- c(4,10,2)

> n[nd]

[1] 17 11 19

You can even utilize indices to remove values from any vector. Following is an example where you give a command to remove value at the 4th position:

> n[-4]

[1] 20 19 18 16 15 14 13 12 11 10 9 8 7 6 5 4 3

[18] 2 1 0

And, in case you wish to remove the initial 15 numbers, then type the following command:

> n[-(1:15)]

[1] 5 4 3 2 1 0

Ways to change values in any vector:

Let' again consider that basketball game example where Philip and George made baskets in five basketball games.

> Phillip.baskets <- c(10,3,3,5,8)

> George.baskets <- c(4,2,1,1,10)

Now, assume that there was an error while noting down the number of baskets made by Phillip. In the 2nd game, Phillip made 6 baskets, not 3. This error can be easily rectified by utilizing indices:

> Phillip.baskets[2] <- 6

> Phillip.baskets

[1] 10 6 3 5 8

Similarly, there were two errors while noting down the number of baskets made by George. In the 3rd and 4th game, he in reality made five baskets. This error can also be easily rectified by utilizing indices:

> George.baskets[c(3,4)] <- 5

> George.baskets

[1] 4 2 5 5 10

These were some of the examples to get values in and out of Vectors. Now, we'll discuss the various ways to work with logical Vectors.

How to work with logical Vectors

We'll talk about the values TRUE and FALSE. These values are called logical values in R. You can perform countless functions with logical values, as you can create vectors which consist of merely logical values. And, you can utilize such logical vectors like an argument to support the index functions, which works as a potent tool.

Ways to compare values:

In order to create logical vectors, you ought to understand the various ways to compare values, and R comes with a collection of operators which anyone can utilize to get the job done. Following is a table of operators:

Operator	Outcome
x == y	Returns TRUE if x exactly equals y
x != y	Returns TRUE if x differs from y
x > y	Returns TRUE if x is larger than y
x >= y	Returns TRUE if x is larger than or exactly equal to y
x < y	Returns TRUE if x is smaller than y
x <= y	Returns TRUE if x is smaller than or exactly equal to y
x & y	Returns the result of x and y
x | y	Returns the result of x or y
! x	Returns not x
xor(x, y)	Returns the result of x xor y (x or y but not x and y)

Let's again consider the basketball game example. Now, in order to confirm the games in which Phillip made less than 4 baskets, just type the following command:

> Phillip.baskets <- c(10,3,3,5,8)

> Phillip.baskets < 4

[1] FALSE TRUE TRUE FALSE FALSE

The outcome reveals the 2nd and 3rd games. Now, in case you've created a very lengthy vector, then to keep a count of numbers could pose a big problem. To tackle such problem, R comes with the **which( )** function. So, to check the games in which Phillip made less than 4 baskets, just type the following code:

> which(Phillip.baskets < 4)

[1] 2 3

Here, the **which( )** function exhibits the indices where the value holds TRUE.

Ways to use logical vectors like indices:

The index function works quite efficiently with the logical vectors. You can utilize these logical vectors to effectively pick certain values from a vector. In case you opt to utilize a logical vector for indexing purposes, R will exhibit a vector with just the values where the logical vector holds TRUE.

Now, in case you wish to know how many baskets Phillip made more than George, just type the following command:

> Total <- Phillip.baskets > George.basket

> Phillip.baskets [Total]

[1] 10 3 3 5

In case you wish to retain only the values bigger than 3 in the vector y, just type the following command:

> y <- c(2, 5, 7, 3)

> y[y > 3]

[1] 5 7

Ways to merge logical statements:

Lets' assume you wish to check, whether or not, a value lies inside a certain parameter. For instance, you wish to know whether it's bigger than the smallest number, and lower than the largest number. One example would be the basketball games in which Phillip made the least or the most baskets. To find the correct results, first try to note the games in which Phillip made the least baskets, and when he made the most baskets:

First of all, construct the following logical vectors:

```
> least.baskets <- Phillip.baskets == least(Phillip.baskets)
> most.baskets <- Phillip.baskets == most(Phillip.baskets)
```

least.baskets will inform you in case the number is equivalent to the least, and most.baskets will inform you in case the number is equivalent to the most.

Merge both of the vectors by using the OR (|) operator:

```
> least.baskets | most.baskets
[1] TRUE TRUE TRUE FALSE FALSE
```

These were some of the ways to work with logical vectors. Next, we'll discuss the various ways use character vectors for Text data, and to manipulate text.

How to use character vectors for Text data, and manipulate text

Character vectors symbolize text in R. A character vector is basically a vector containing characters.

Ways to create as well as assign named vectors:

You need to utilize the assignment operator (<-) for the purpose of assigning names to any vectors. Let's assume that you wish to construct a named vector for all the days in every month. You need to construct a numeric vector consisting of the total count of days in every month. After that, utilize the in-built data-set called 'month.name' to name the months:

> days.month.count <- c(31, 28, 31, 30, 31, 30, 31, 31, 30, 31, 30, 31)

> title(days.month.count) <- month.name

> days.month.count

Jan Feb March April May June July August Sept Oct Nov Dec

31 28 31   30   31   30   31   31   30   31 30 31

You can even utilize the above-mentioned vector to get the month with 30 days:

> title(days.month.count [days.month.count ==30])

[1] "April" "June" "Sept" "Nov"

The result shows name of the months with 30 days.

Ways to manipulate text:

A set of merged letters or/and words is known as a 'string'. In case you wish to manipulate the text, you must be able to either split the letters, or merge them.

How to split text

Construct a character vector by the name sp, and assign it "I love to play hockey":

> sp <- "I love to play hockey"

> sp

[1] "I love to play hockey"

Now, in order to split the above text at the spaces, you need to utilize **strsplit( )** function:

> strsplit(sp, " ")

[[1]]

[1] "I" "love" "to" "play" "hockey"

The result shows the string split.

How to concatenate text

In order to concatenate text, you need to utilize the **paste( )** function:

paste("I", "love", "to", "play", "hockey")

[1] "I love to play hockey"

The **paste()** automatically utilizes any blank space it encounters to combine the vectors.

These were some of the ways to use character vectors for Text data, and manipulate text. Now, we'll discuss the various ways to work with dates and times.

How to work with dates and times

R comes with a variety of functions which permit you to experiment with dates and times. The simplest technique for constructing a date is to utilize the **as.Date( )** function. For instance, you write the inaugural day of the 2016 Rio Olympic Games as:

> og <- as.Date("2016-08-05")

> og

[1] "2016-08-05"

> str(og)

Date[1:1], format: "2016-08-05"

And, if you wish to know which weekday this date falls on, you need to utilize **weekdays( )** function:

> weekdays(og)

[1] "Friday"

You can even subtract or add values from dates to build fresh dates. For instance, to compute the date which is 8 days after this, type the following code:

```
> og + 8
[1] "2016-08-13"
```

Just like in case of text and/or numbers, you can place many dates inside any vector. To build a vector of 6 days beginning on August 5, add 0:5 to the initial date.

```
> og + 0:5
[1] "2016-08-05" "2016-08-06" "2016-08-07" "2016-08-08"
[5] "2016-08-09" "2016-08-10"
```

Below is the table of some helpful Functions with Dates:

Function	Description
as.Date()	Converts character string to Date
weekdays()	Full weekday name in the current locale (for example, Sunday, Monday, Tuesday)
months()	Full month name in the current locale (for example, January, February, March)
quarters()	Quarter numbers (Q1, Q2, Q3, or Q4)
seq()	Generates dates sequences if you pass it a Date object as its first argument

Ways to incorporate time details to dates:

Sometimes, just dates aren't sufficient. You're also required to designate a precise time. So, to denote time details along with dates, you can pick any one of these functions:

- **as.POSIXct()**
- **as.POSIXlt()**

The above- mentioned date-time functions relatively vary, as these stock-up the date related data internally, in addition to the technique by which a user can get the date as well as time values.

Below is table which lists some of the formatting codes which are helpful when you try to incorporate time details to dates.

80

Format	Details
%H	Hours as a decimal number (00–23)
%I	Hours as a decimal number (01–12)
%M	Minutes as a decimal number (00–59)
%S	Seconds as a decimal number (00–61)
%p	AM/PM indicator

These were some of the ways to work with dates and times. Next, we'll talk about the various ways to combine Vectors into Matrix.

How to combine Vectors into Matrix

Until now, we've been creating vectors to store data in a 1-D (one-dimensional) arrangement. However, besides vectors, R also offers to work with matrices. In reality, R actually excels with its matrix computations and operations.

Vectors are very much associated to a larger group of entities known as 'arrays'. Arrays come with two very significant attributes:

- They hold just a particular type of value.
- They possess dimensions.

Now, the number of dimensions actually establishes the array type. A vector has just one dimension, a matrix has two dimensions, and an array has in excess of two dimensions.

How to create matrix

You just need to utilize the **matrix()** function, to create a matrix. However, you need to provide some details to R first, such as which values you wish to place inside the matrix, and how you wish to place those values. The **matrix()** function comes with certain arguments to manage this:

- data means a vector of values which you wish to place inside the matrix.
- ncol accepts a solo number and informs R about the number of columns you desire.
- nrow accepts a solo number and informs R about the number of rows you desire.
- byrow accepts a logical value and informs R in case you wish to load the matrix column by column, or row by row.

The below mentioned command displays a matrix with the numbers from 2 to 13 in 3 columns and 4 rows:

```
> fm <- matrix(2:13, ncol=3)

> fm

     [,1] [,2] [,3]

[1,]  2    6   10

[2,]  3    7   11

[3,]  4    8   12

[4,]  5    9   13
```

Now, you don't need to state both the ncol or/and nrow. Even if you state just one, R automatically interprets about the other. And, in case you wish to load the matrix row wise:

```
> matrix(2:13, ncol=3, byrow=TRUE)

     [,1] [,2] [,3]

[1,]  2    3    4

[2,]  5    6    7

[3,]  8    9   10

[4,] 11   12   13
```

Ways to combine vectors into a matrix:

Let's again consider the example of the basketball game, where we created two vectors consisting of number of baskets made by Phillip and George. Now, in case you wish to put the number of baskets made by both of them in a single entity, you can utilize matrices. You need to merge both the vectors like 2 rows of a matrix using the **rbind( )** function:

> **Phillip.baskets <- c(10,3,3,5,8)**

> **George.baskets <- c(4,2,1,1,10)**

> **Total.baskets <- rbind(Phillip.baskets, George.baskets)**

Here, the entity Total.baskets is a matrix, and the rows acquire the vector's names.

> **Total.baskets**

	[,1]	[,2]	[,3]	[,4]	[,5]
Phillip.baskets	10	3	3	5	8
George.baskets	4	2	1	1	10

Likewise, to merge the vectors as columns of a matrix, you need to utilize the **cbind( )** function:

> **cbind(2:4, 5:7, matrix(8:13, ncol=2))**

```
     [,1] [,2] [,3] [,4]
[1,]  2    5    8   11
[2,]  3    6    9   12
[3,]  4    7   10   13
```

In the above example, you merged 3 different anonymous entities:

- A vector with the values 2:4
- A vector with the values 5:7
- And, a matrix with 3 rows and 2 columns, loaded column by column with the values 8 to 13.

Now, the above example exhibits various helpful properties of **rbind( )** & **cbind( )** functions:

- These work with both matrices as well as vectors.
- You can provide in excess of 2 arguments to each function.
- You can merge diverse types of entities, provided that the dimensions are appropriate.

How to calculate with matrices

Possibly the strongest attribute of R is its ability to handle complicated matrix calculations in a very simple way. So, when you consider calculations on matrices, you can either consider its elements, or the entire matrix as a value. In case you wish to add scalar (a solo number) to any matrix, you integrate that solo number to each constituent of that matrix. You just need to utilize the addition (+) operator, to perform this:

```
> fm + 5

     [,1] [,2] [,3]
[1,]  7   11   15
[2,]  8   12   16
[3,]  9   13   17
[4,] 10   14   18
```

Likewise, you can even utilize numerous arithmetic operators to carry out any calculation on each of the elements of a matrix. Consider one more example:

In the above- mentioned matrix fm, you wish to add 2 to the 1st row, 3 to the 2nd row, 4 to the 3rd row, and 5 to the 4th row. This can be done by creating another matrix fx, which consists of

3 columns and 4 rows, and has 2, 3, 4 and 5 as values in the 1st, 2nd, 3rd and 4th rows, in that order:

> fx <- matrix(2:5, nrow=4, ncol=3)

Utilizing the addition (+) operator, both the matrices (fm & fx) can be merged:

```
> fm + fx
      [,1]  [,2]  [,3]
[1,]   4    8     12
[2,]   6    10    14
[3,]   8    12    16
[4,]   10   14    18
```

You need to keep in mind that the dimension of the two matrices should match. Or, R won't perform the operation, and you'll get the following outcome:

```
> fm + fx[,2:4]

Error in fm + fx[, 2:4] : non-conformable arrays
```

However, in case if we add a vector as an alternative to a matrix, you'll get the following outcome:

> **fm + 2:4**

```
       [,1]  [,2]  [,3]
[1,]    4     8    12
[2,]    6    10    14
[3,]    8    12    16
[4,]   10    14    18
```

Here, R considers the matrix like a vector, and plainly overlooks the dimensions.

These were some of the ways to calculate with matrices. Now, we'll talk about the various ways to combine different types of value in a Data-Frame, and manipulate those values.

How to combine different types of value in a Data-Frame, and manipulate those values

Data-sets are developed from diverse data types. For instance, you can include your employee's names, their incomes, and their joining date, all in the similar data-set. However, you just can't merge all such data in a single matrix without changing the data to a character value. Therefore, you require a new data-structure to retain all such details in R. And, this data-structure is known as a Data-Frame.

Ways to build a data-frame from a matrix:

Let's again consider the basketball game example, where we built a matrix Total.baskets which contained the number of baskets made by Phillip and George:

Total.baskets

	[,1]	[,2]	[,3]	[,4]	[,5]
Phillip	10	3	3	5	8
George	4	2	1	1	10

We can convert this matrix into a data-frame having 2 variables: one variable with Phillip's baskets and another variable with George's baskets. Now, to transform the Total.baskets matrix into a data-frame, you need to utilize the **as.data.frame( )** function:

```
> dt.baskets <- as.data.frame(t(Total.baskets))
```

Here, we also need to utilize the transpose **t( )** function, to build a data frame. The **t()** function flips the matrix, which turns rows into columns and vice versa. In the case of data-frames, every variable means a column; however, in the Total.baskets matrix, the rows symbolize the number of baskets for a solo participant. Hence, to facilitate the preferred outcome, you need to flip the Total.baskets matrix with **t( )** function prior to transforming it into a data-frame using **as.data.frame()** function. Following is the result:

> **dt.baskets**

	Phillip	George
1st	10	4
2nd	3	2
3rd	3	1
4th	5	1
5th	8	10

You can even utilize the **str()** function to check the internal composition of the output:

> str(dt.baskets)

'data.frame': 5 obs. of 2 variables:

$ Phillip: num 10 3 3 5 8

$ George: num 4 2 1 1 10

Hence, it is confirmed that it's a real data-set.

Other way to create a data-frame:

The previous method to create a data-frame from a matrix cannot be utilized to create a data-frame from diverse value types. You need to utilize the **data.frame( )** function in order to create a data-frame from any other value types.

Let's create a small data-frame containing names, incomes, and joining dates of small number of employees. You need to build 3 separate vectors with the essential details which are as follows:

> names <- c('Peter Parker', 'Clark Kent', 'Bruce Wayne')

> income <- c(31000, 19000, 25000)

```
> dt.join <- as.Date(c('2012-10-5','2009-4-14','2005-6-
20'))
```

Here, you possess 3 diverse vectors:

- **Character vector** (employee names)
- **Numeric vector** (income)
- **Date vector** (date of joining)

Now, you merge all these 3 vectors into a data-frame. Type the following command:

```
> dt.emp <- data.frame(names, income, dt.join)
```

The following is the outcome of this code:

```
> str(dt.emp)
```

'data.frame': 3 objects. 3 variables:

$ names: Factor w/ 3 levels "Peter Parker" "Clark Kent" "Bruce Wayne"

$ income: num 31000, 19000, 25000

$ dt.join: Date, format: "2012-10-5" "2009-4-14" "2005-6-20"

Manipulating Values in a Data Frame:

Constructing a data-frame is pleasant; however, data-frames are relatively worthless in case you're not able to alter its values, or integrate data to the data-frames. Fortunately, data-frames come with certain good features. In case you wish to manipulate the values, nearly all the ploys you performed on matrices could be utilized on the data-frames too. Additionally, you can even utilize certain techniques which are exclusively designed to be carried out for data-frames.

How to extract values from data-frame

In several scenarios, you'd be able to extract values from any data-frame by assuming that the data-frame is a matrix, and by utilizing the methods you performed on matrices. However, quite dissimilar to both matrices as well as arrays, data-frames are not at all vectors. So always bear in mind that, data-frames are lists of vectors, and even though they might appear as matrices, they actually are not.

Assuming data-frames as a matrix:

Let's again consider the basketball game example. We'll utilize the data-frame **dt.baskets** which we built in the "Ways to build a data-frame from a matrix" section earlier.

> **dt.baskets**

	Phillip	**George**
1st	**10**	**4**
2nd	**3**	**2**
3rd	**3**	**1**
4th	**5**	**1**
5th	**8**	**10**

Now, you can extract the count of baskets made by Phillip in the 4th game:

> **dt.baskets['4th', 'Phillip']**

[1] 5

Similarly, you can extract the entire baskets made by George utilizing the column index:

```
> dt.baskets[, 2]
```

[1] 4 2 1 1 10

And, in case you wish to see the results to be like a data-frame, then you need to utilize drop=FALSE:

```
> str(dt.baskets[, 2, drop=FALSE])
```

'data.frame': 5 obs. of 1 variable:

$ George: num 4 2 1 1 10

Now, you might have noticed the dollar symbol ($). This symbol is merely a precise approach to access various variables. And, to access the George variable, you need to utilize the dollar symbol in the following way:

```
> dt.baskets$George
```

[1] 4 2 1 1 10

The result here displays a vector with the entire values within that variable. These were some of the ways to combine different types of value in a Data-Frame, and manipulate those values. Now, we'll discuss how to create a list, and combine different objects in it.

How to create a List, and combine different objects in it

Data-frames are lists of vectors, and even though they might appear as matrices, they actually are not. A list is a relatively common and flexible kind of entity in R. These can be really useful for the purpose of grouping diverse forms of entities, or to perform computations on an entire set of diverse entities.

How to create a list

To create a list, you need to utilize the **list( )** function, and you can do it in two ways. You can either build an unnamed list or a named list. Now, the dissimilarity is minute; in both cases, consider a list like a huge box loaded with number of sacks consisting of all types of diverse objects. And, instead of numbering all such sacks, if these are being named, then what you possess in the end is a named list.

Ways to create an unnamed list:

To construct an unnamed list is pretty simple as you need to utilize the **list( )** function, and insert all the entities, you wish in that list, just within the ( ). Let's again consider the basketball game example where we built a matrix Total.baskets which contained the number of baskets made by Phillip and George:

Total.baskets

	1st	2nd	3rd	4th	5th
Phillip	10	3	3	5	8
George	4	2	1	1	10

Now, in case you wish to merge the above matrix with a character vector representing the year, you need to type the following code:

```
> l.baskets <- list(Total.baskets, '2015-2016')
> l.baskets
[[1]]
```

	1st	2nd	3rd	4th	5th
Phillip	10	3	3	5	8
George	4	2	1	1	10

```
[[2]]
[1] "2015-2016"
```

Here, the entity l.baskets has 2 elements: Total.baskets (the matrix) and 2015-2016 (the year). The numeric values within the symbol [[|]] signifies the 'sack number' of every element.

Ways to create a named list:

To build a named (or labeled) list, you just need to add the names right before the values, just within the ( ) symbol of the list( ) function:

> nl.baskets <- list(counts=Total.baskets, year='2015-2016')

The following would be the result:

> nl.baskets

$ counts

	1st	2nd	3rd	4th	5th
Phillip	10	3	3	5	8
George	4	2	1	1	10

$ year

[1] "2015-2016"

98

Here, the $ symbol signifies the name of the list of elements.

Ways to combine lists:

To combine the lists, all you require is a function which we have frequently utilized earlier, the **c( )** function. This function can merge diverse types of entities and, hence, can be utilized to combine lists, and create a fresh list.

Now, in case you wish to add the details about the competitors, you need to make a list first. And, to ensure that you get the similar results, you need to reconstruct the original l.baskets:

> **l.baskets <- list(Total.baskets,'2015-2016')**

> **competitors <- list(rownames(Total.baskets))**

After that, you need to merge the competitors list with the l.baskets list, utilizing the **c( )** function:

> **c(l.baskets, competitors)**

[[1]]

	1st	2nd	3rd	4th	5th
Phillip	10	3	3	5	8
George	4	2	1	1	10

[[2]]

[1]   "2015-2016"

[[3]]

[1]   "Phillip" "George"

The result exhibits a combination of all the different lists. These were some of the ways to create a list, and combine different entities in it.

****

In this chapter, we discussed the various ways getting started working in R. We covered diverse topics such as fundamentals of arithmetic, how to organize data in Vectors, how to work with logical vectors, manipulating text, vector & matrix, data frames, and creation of lists.

In the next chapter, we'll talk about how to effectively Code in R.

Chapter Five: How to effectively Code in R

In this chapter, we'll talk about how to effectively Code in R. We'll discuss how to efficiently automate your work by utilizing functions, how to utilize arguments the smart way, how to control the Logical Flow, how to loop through different values, and how to effectively debug your Code.

How to efficiently automate your work by utilizing functions

To efficiently automate you work in R you can utilize its in-built functions. However, R permits you to create your own custom functions which are very easy to build. Let's just create a function:

Script creation:

Assume that you wish to display fractional digits just like percentages, which are rounded numbers. Just type the following command in your console:

y <- c(0.367, 2.7742, 0.93223)

c <- round(y * 100, digits = 1)

```
z <- paste(c, "%", sep = "")

print(z)
```

In case you save this script-file as a xyz.R, you just need to call this script-file utilizing the **source( )** function:

```
> source('xyz.R')

[1] "36.7%" "277.4%" "93.2%"
```

Ways to transform a script:

To transform the above script into a function, you have to perform certain small steps. Consider the script as a manufacturing unit which accepts the raw materials and furnishes them. Now, to construct your manufacturing unit, just modify your script like this:

```
m.unit <- function(y) {

c <- round(y * 100, digits = 1)

z <- paste(c, "%", sep = "")

return(z)

}
```

The various elements of the function created above are as follows:

- The keyword 'function' ought to be followed by brackets (parentheses). It informs R about the arrival of a function.
- The brackets (parentheses) following the function store a list of arguments. Here it is y.
- The symbols { } means the body of your function.
- The **return( )** function displays the result. Here, you're allowed to insert just one item within the brackets (parentheses).

And, most importantly, you need to utilize the assignment (<-) operator to assign the entire function in an entity (here its m.unit). Now, the above function owns a pleasant name, and is all set to be utilized.

How to utilize the function

Just like in the script creation stage, you need to save the script first, and then utilize the **source( )** function to get the output displayed on your console. However, you'll see no results, as R won't permit you to know that it has actually loaded the function. Now, in reality, the function do exist in the workspace, and you can verify it by utilizing the **ls( )** function:

> ls( )

[1] "m.unit" "c" "z" "y"

These were some of the ways to efficiently automate your work by utilizing functions. Next, we'll talk about the ways to utilize arguments the smart way.

How to utilize arguments the smart way

In the previous example, the **m.unit( )** function multiplies the stated digits by one hundred, which actually works good, in case you wish to transform fractional digits into percentages. However, in case, the stated digits are just percentages and not fractional digits, then you're required to divide the stated digits by one hundred to obtain the accurate outcome:

> p <- c(36.7, 277.4, 93.2)

> m(p/100)

[1] "36.7%" "277.4%" "93.2%"

Now, you can actually perform the similar step by adding one more argument to the function which manages the multiplication feature. Following is the way to do it:

How to add the 'multiply' argument

You can add additional arguments by putting them within the brackets (parentheses) following the keyword 'function'. Each argument should be separated by a comma. So, in order to add 'multiply' as an argument, which controls the multiplication feature in the code, you need to type the following:

```
m.unit <- function(y, multiply){

c <- round(y * muliply, digits = 1)

paste(c, "%", sep = "")

}
```

Here, you can state the 'multiply' argument when you call the m.unit( ). And, in case you wish to utilize the p vector from the previous section, you need to type the following:

```
> m.unit(p, multiply = 1)

[1] "36.7%" "277.4%" "93.2%"
```

How to add any default value

The option to add an additional argument provides you with further control over that function; however, it props up a new trouble. In case, you don't state the 'multiply' argument in the above mentioned **m.uint( )** function, the following would be the outcome:

> **> m.unit(new.numbers)**

Error in y * multiply: 'multiply' is missing

As you didn't state the 'multiply' argument, R couldn't understand the argument; consequently, it displays an error message and asks you for further details. Now, this could be really frustrating as this also means that you would need to state multiply=100 each time you utilize the function. Here, stating a default value for the 'multiply' argument will definitely help you out.

You need to state the default values (regarding any argument) by utilizing the (=) sign, followed by the default value. Just type the following command:

```
m.unit <- function(y, multiply = 100){

c <- round(y * multiply, digits = 1)

paste(c, "%", sep = " ")

}
```

These were some of the ways to utilize arguments the smart way. Now, we'll talk about the ways to control the Logical Flow.

How to control the Logical Flow

A function is merely a plain series of actions; however, these are extremely rigid as well. And quite frequently, you may wish to have choices and conduct action on the basis of a definite value.

Utilizing the 'if' statements:

Now, to describe a choice in the R code is very easy: If a certain condition holds true, then it will perform a definite chore. Numerous programming languages allow you to perform that precisely with 'if . . . then' words. In R it's way simpler. You just need to remove the word 'then' and indicate your choice utilizing the 'if' statement.

An 'if' statement has 3 constituents:

- Keyword 'if'.
- A solo logical value within the brackets (parentheses).
- A code segment within { } (braces) which will be carried out if the logical value holds TRUE.

Let's just write a little function and name it **pCal( )**, which computes the rate that you charge to a client on the basis of the hours you worked for that client. Just type the following:

```
pCal <- function(hrs, rh=30){

np <- hrs * rh

round(np)

}
```

Following is the description of the code:

- The keyword 'function' describes the function.
- The code within the { } (braces) is the function's main body.
- Within the brackets (parentheses), you need to state the arguments hrs (hours) and rh (here the default value is $30 per/hour).

- You compute the np (total charges) by multiplying 'hrs' & 'rh'.
- The final result will be the rounded number (total charges).

Now, assume that there are certain clients who provide you with loads of work, and you make a decision to offer them a 10 % discount, on the rates you charge per hour, for the jobs with over 110 hours of time. Subsequently, in case the number of working hours is in excess of 110 hours times, then you're needed to compute the fresh price by multiplying 0.9 with the total charges. Following is the code:

```
pCal <- function(hrs, rh=30){

np <- hrs * rh

if(hrs > 110) {

np <- np * 0.9

}

round(np)

}
```

Here, the discount is only available when the number of working hours is in excess of 110 hours of time. Following are the different output examples:

```
> pCal(hours = 45)

[1] 1350

> pCal(hours = 120)

[1] 3240
```

Utilizing the 'if...else' statements:

In certain scenarios, you would want the function to perform a certain task if a specific condition holds true, and to perform some other task if the condition doesn't hold true. And, although you'd be able to perform this with 'if' statements, there is certainly a simpler method to do this by utilizing the 'if...else' statement. This statement consists of the similar constituents like the 'if' statement, and some additional ones:

- The 'else' keyword is put below the 1st code section.
- The 2nd code section written between { } (braces), has to be performed only in case the outcome of the condition in the 1st section (the if( ) statement) returns FALSE.

Let's consider an example. In certain countries, the sum of VAT (value added tax) which is needed to be paid on specific services is based on whether the consumer is a public or a private establishment. Just assume that public establishments need to shell-out only 6 % VAT, and private establishments need to shell-out 12 % VAT. Now, you can include an additional argument 'private' to the previous pCal( ) function, and type the following command to add the accurate total of VAT:

```
pCal <- function(hrs, rh=30, private=TRUE){

np <- hrs * rh

if(hrs > 110) np <- np * 0.9

if(private) {

tp <- np * 1.12

} else {

tp <- np * 1.06

}

round(tp)

}
```

Now, in case you worked for 35 hours, the results would be different VAT charges for public and private establishments:

```
> pCal(35, private=TRUE)
```

[1] 1176

> pCal(35, private=FALSE)

[1] 1113

These were some of the ways to control the Logical Flow. Next, we'll talk about how to loop through different values.

How to loop through different values

Ways to create a 'for loop':

Just like in several other programming languages, a 'for loop' is being utilized to replicate a certain task for each vector value. Following is the way a 'for loop' is created in R:

for(x in values){

... Perform a task...

}

Following are the constituents of this 'for loop':

- The 'for' keyword, which is followed by brackets (parentheses).
- A variable within the brackets (parentheses). Here, we've used 'x'.
- The variable 'x' is followed by the 'in' keyword.
- A vector containing 'values' to loop through.
- A section of code within the { } (braces), which is required to be performed for each value in the vector 'values'.

In the code section, you can utilize the variable 'x'. Every occasion when R loops through the code, it allocates the subsequent value in the vector containing 'values', to the variable 'x.

How to compute values in a 'for loop'

Let's again consider the example of the **pCal( )** function. In the previous example, we calculated how to charge different VAT for public and private establishments. Here, we'll tell you how to utilize a 'for loop' to calculate the charges for many clients, instantly. Just type the following code:

```
pCal <- function(hrs, rh=30, customer){
np <- hrs * rh *
```

```
                    ifelse(hrs > 110, 0.9, 1)

V <- numeric(0)

for(x in customer){

    V <- c(V,switch(x, private=1.12, public=1.06, 1))

}

tp <- np * V

round(tp)

}
```

The initial and the final part of the **pCal( )** function doesn't change; however, in the central block, you perform the following:

- Build 'numeric' vector with '0' value, and named it as 'V'.
- For each of the value in the vector 'customer', you applied **switch( )** function to choose the right sum of Value Added Tax to be paid.
- In every circle through the loop, you added the result of **switch( )** function in the vector 'V'.

The final outcome is a vector 'V' which possess the right figures of the Value Added Tax, for every customer. These were some of the ways to loop through different values. Next, we'll talk about how to effectively debug your Code.

How to effectively debug your Code

No one can write a perfect code devoid of any errors. Therefore, rather than speculating about the mistakes in your code, you first step must be to inquire to yourself, where have you committed those errors?

Understanding where the problem lies:

Here, a bug is just a different word for an error in your code. Hence, the debugging process doesn't engage any pesticides. It literally means removing every form of 'logical' or/and 'semantic' errors in your program.

Therefore, prior to removing those bugs, you need to understand the stuff you're searching for. Following are some of the different categories of errors:

- **'Syntax' errors:** If you've written a code which R can't interpret, then you have committed 'syntax' errors. The outcome of such errors is always an error message, and it frequently happens due to some misspelling, or incomplete bracket.
- **'Semantic' errors:** If you've written a code which doesn't perform the intended task, then you have committed a 'semantic' error. Here, although the

code is proper, however, the results are not what it was meant for, and your code is unsuccessful.

- **'Logical' errors:** Such types of errors are perhaps the toughest to search for. Here, the code works fine, and it doesn't display any type of warning or error; however, it doesn't exhibit the expected outcome. The real fault is not actually in the code, it lies in the logic it implements.

Now, all this might appear like minute information; however, searching for different kinds of bugs needs diverse tactics. You can simply trace any 'syntax' error by simply understanding the error messages; however, tracing a 'semantic' error could lead to an entirely different level of hardship, and 'logical' errors might give you nightmares, as you simply won't know about their existence.

Interpreting warnings and errors:

In case anything is erroneous with your code, R will inform you in the following ways:

- First, the code will run till the end, and after it's completed, R will return a warning message.
- The code ends instantly as R can't perform it, and R returns an error message.

When you're able to interpret warnings and errors, you can swiftly understand what went wrong.

Browsing through the function:

In case, you opt for the 'browser mode', you can verify your R code to confirm the status of the different entities. You need to utilize the following commands:

- Type '**n**' and press '**Enter**' key to run the subsequent line of code.
- You're not required to type '**n**' anymore in order to run the succeeding lines of code line wise. You just keep pressing '**Enter**'.
- To run the residual portion of your code, you need to type '**c**' and then press 'Enter' key.
- If you wish to exit the 'browser mode', just type '**Q**' and then press 'Enter' key.

These were some of the ways to effectively debug your code.

*****

In this chapter, we discussed how to effectively Code in R.

In the next chapter, we'll talk about the various ways to efficiently manipulate your data.

Chapter Six: How to efficiently manipulate your data

In this chapter, we'll talk about the various ways to efficiently manipulate your data. We'll discuss how to get your data in & out of R, how to effectively manipulate and process your data, and how to summarize your data.

How to get your data in & out of R

As a user, you'll have numerous alternatives for getting your data into R. As spreadsheets are very popular, we'll start with importing data from spreadsheets. The figure below is a little spreadsheet displaying the periodic table of the 1st 10 elements. We'll use this spreadsheet as an example throughout this section.

Periodic Table (First Ten Elements)

	Atomic number	Name	Symbol	Group	Period	Block	State at STP	Occurrence	Description
1									
2	1	Hydrogen	H	1	1	s	Gas	Primordial	Non-metal
3	2	Helium	He	18	1	s	Gas	Primordial	Noble gas
4	3	Lithium	Li	1	2	s	Solid	Primordial	Alkali metal
5	4	Beryllium	Be	2	2	s	Solid	Primordial	Alkaline earth metal
6	5	Boron	B	13	2	p	Solid	Primordial	Metalloid
7	6	Carbon	C	14	2	p	Solid	Primordial	Non-metal
8	7	Nitrogen	N	15	2	p	Gas	Primordial	Non-metal
9	8	Oxygen	O	16	2	p	Gas	Primordial	Non-metal
10	9	Fluorine	F	17	2	p	Gas	Primordial	Halogen
11	10	Neon	Ne	18	2	p	Gas	Primordial	Noble gas

How to enter data in the R text-editor

Even though R is mostly used as a language for programming purposes, it comes with a relatively basic data-editor, which lets you to enter your data straight into R, utilizing the **edit( )** function. Now, to utilize the R text-editor, you're required to start a variable first. For instance, to construct a data-frame and physically enter a bit of the data in the periodic table, just type:

elm <- data.frame( )

elm <- edit(elm)

The code will return an interactive text-editor (the figure below), where you can manually type your data.

R Text Editor

	var1	var2	var3	var4
1	1	Hydrogen	H	
2	2	Helium		
3	3	Lithium		
4				

You can scroll up & down, or left & right. However, the text-editor won't permit you to change the names of rows & columns. Now, you can enter a little data, and save the work by clicking on the 'X' in the right-top corner of the editor. And, to see the particulars which you've just typed, you can utilize the **print( )** function:

> print(elm)

	var1	var2	var3
1	1	Hydrogen	H
2	2	Helium	He
3	3	Lithium	Li

121

How to utilize the 'Clipboard' for the copy and paste purpose

One more technique to import data into R is to utilize the 'Clipboard' for copying and pasting the data. You have to utilize the **readClipboard( )** function, if you wish to import data from 'Clipboard'. For instance, first select the cells B3:B5 in the spreadsheet (periodic table), after that press '**Ctrl+C**' keys to copy the selected cells into the 'Clipboard', and then type the following code:

> **> a <- readClipboard( )**

> **> a**

> **[1] "Helium" "Lithium" "Beryllium"**

And, if you wish to import data in the tabular form, you can utilize the **read.table()** function. You can modify the **read.table( )** function by altering its arguments. The arguments are as follows:

- **file:** It means the filename to be imported. In case the filename is PD, then state file= "PD".
- **sep:** It means the separator which separates the data elements. Regarding the 'MS Excel' spreadsheet data, the tab (denoted by "\t") is the separator.

- **header:** It simply denotes, whether or not, the 'Clipboard' data has a header in the initial row (in other words the names of the column).

First, select the cells A1:D5 in the spreadsheet (periodic table), after that press '**Ctrl+C**' keys to copy the selected cells. Afterwards, just type the following code:

> rt <- read.table(file = "PD", sep = "\t", header=FALSE)

> rt

```
1    Hydrogen    H    1
2    Helium      He   1
3    Lithium     Li   1
4    Beryllium   Be   2
```

How to export your data out of R

To get your data out of R in order to paste it somewhere else, you need to utilize the **writeClipboard( )** function, or the **write.table( ) function**. Now, **writeClipboard( )** is quite effective, if you want to export vector data. For instance, in order to export the titles of the in-built data-set by the name 'iris', just type:

> writeClipboard(titles(iris))

The code won't return any result; however, you can definitely paste the vector in a spreadsheet. Below is figure of the spreadsheet when you paste the vector into Excel-sheet. **Note:** The in-built data-sets in R, are recognized in the similar way as functions are recognized. To know more about it just type: **?Iris**.

To export the data in a tabular form, you have to utilize the **write.table( )** function. Again, this won't return any result; however, you can definitely paste it into any spreadsheet just like in the case of **writeClipboard( )** function . These were some of the ways to get your data in & out of R. Now, we'll discuss various ways to effectively manipulate and process your data.

Effective ways to manipulate and process your data:

Now, the time has come to utilize each and every tool which you studied in the previous chapters. You possess a full understanding of how to import & export data from R, you understand how to utilize lists as well as data-frames, and you also can write functions now. All these tools, when merged together, form the fundamental arsenal to manipulate and process your data in R.

Ways to choose the most fitting data-structure:

The initial choice you need to consider prior to evaluating your data is how to symbolize your data in R. In the previous chapters, you learned that the essential data-structures in R, are matrices, vectors, data-frames, and lists.

In case your data is one dimensional only, then you do recognize that vectors symbolize such data type fairly well. But, in case your data is multi- dimensional, then you possess the option of utilizing data-frames, lists, or matrices. Now, the real issue is: When to utilize which?

Matrices as well as multi-dimensional arrays are helpful when your entire data are of a solo category, which means either characters or numeric. If you're familiar with subjects like statistics or mathematics, then you're not new to matrices.

However, in several realistic circumstances, you'll have data with various diverse categories. You'll have a combination of character as well as numeric data. Here, you have to utilize either data-frames or lists.

In case you assume that your data is like a spreadsheet, a data-frame is perhaps a fine option. Bear in mind that a data-frame is merely a list of vectors with names that are of the similar length, which is theoretically quite related to a spreadsheet with column headings. If you're well acquainted with databases, then you can consider a data-frame just like a solo database table. Data-frames are extremely helpful and, in numerous scenarios, it'll be your first pick for the data storage purpose.

In case your data contains a set of entities and you're simply not able to symbolize that as a data-frame or a matrix, then your best option would be a list. As lists can hold every type of other entities, which includes data-frames or even other lists, these are extremely flexible.

Hence, R comes with an extensive range of tools to process your data. The following table consists of a synopsis of all the above- mentioned options.

Entity	Details	Remarks
Vector	The basic data object in R, consisting of one or more values of a single type (for example, character, number, or integer).	Think of this as a single column or row in a spreadsheet, or a column in a database table.
Matrix	A multidimensional object of a single type (known as atomic). A matrix is an array of two dimensions.	When you have to store numbers in many dimensions, use arrays.
List	Lists can contain objects of any type.	Lists are very useful for storing collections of data that belong together. Because lists can contain lists, this type of object is very useful.
Data-frame	Data frames are a special kind of named list where all the elements have the same length.	Data frames are similar to a single spreadsheet or to a table in a database.

Knowing the 3 basic subset operators:

Following are the 3 basic subset operators:

- **$:** The $ (dollar) symbol operator picks a solo constituent of your data and confiscates its dimensions. If you utilize it with a data-frame, the outcome will certainly be a vector; if you utilize it with a list (which is named), you obtain that particular constituent.
- **[[:** This operator also returns a solo constituent of your data; however, it provides you with the options of referring to the constituents by their respective positions, instead of by their names. You can utilize it for lists as well as data-frames.

127

- **[**: This special operator can return various constituents of your data.

Knowing the 5 methods of specifying the subset:

In case you utilize the ([) operator, it'll return various constituents of your data. It implies that you require an accurate method to indicate precisely which constituents of your data you want. The following table displays the 5 methods of specifying which constituents of your data you wish to choose or drop. We're utilizing the in-built data-set by the name 'islands' (a named numeric-vector with 48 constituents).

Subset	Outcome	Illustration
Blank	Returns all your data	islands[]
Positive numerical values	Extracts the elements at these locations	islands[c(8, 1, 1, 42)]
Negative numerical values	Extract all but these elements; in other words, excludes these elements	islands[-(3:46)]
Logical values	A logical value of TRUE includes element; FALSE excludes element	islands[islands < 20]
Text strings	Includes elements where the names match	islands[c("Madagascar", "Cuba")]

After going through the system for building subsets, you know how to attempt it with some data-frames. You only need to keep in mind that a data-frame is a two-dimensional entity and consists of columns and rows. It implies that you have to state the subset for rows as well as columns separately.

128

How to summarize your data

As R programming was specifically created to carry-out statistical calculations, you can implement all the frequent statistical methods with a solo command. Furthermore, all such commands are splendidly acknowledged in the 'R Help-files'. And, in case you require further advanced techniques, or to apply progressive research, then there might be a package available for that, and various such packages are accompanied by a guide of examples.

Beginning with the correct data:

Prior to making an attempt to explain your data, you need to ensure that your data is in the correct format. It means:

- Ensuring that your entire data is stored in a data-frame or in a vector (in case your data is a solo variable).
- Make certain that the entire variables are of the right category.
- Verifying that the entire values are processed properly.

Ways to count unique values:

Let's consider the example of the in-built data-set 'mtcars'. It explains the fuel usage and 10 diverse designs of thirty cars from the seventies. It consists of eleven variables which are all numeric. In case, you have no knowledge about the number of diverse values that a variable possesses, you can extract such details in 2 easy steps:

- Obtain the exclusive variable values by utilizing **unique( )** function.
- Obtain the length of the resultant vector by utilizing **length( )** function.

However, in case you utilize the **sapply( )** function, you'll be able to perform this for the entire data-frame. You implement an unknown function merging both the above stated steps on the entire data-frame, just by typing the following:

> sapply(mtcars, k(y) length(unique(y)))

cyl mpg hp disp wt drat qsec vs am carb gr

4 21 19 25 28 22 30 2 2 5 4

Ways to prepare data:

In several real-life scenarios, you're sometimes loaded with plenty of data in a huge box file, and unluckily in such a format, which you can't utilize by any means. However, with the help of R, you can swiftly design your data precisely the way you desire it to be. Simply choosing the variables you require and converting these to the correct format, will be relatively simple.

Let's set up the data-frame 'mtcars' by utilizing certain easy tricks. Build a data-frame 'r':

```
> r <- mtcars[c(3, 1, 11, 8, 9)]

> r$gr <- ord(r$gr)

> r$am <- factor(r$am, labels=c('at', 'mn'))
```

Following is the break-up of the code:

- Pick 4 variables from the data-frame 'mtcars' and store them in a data-frame 'r'.
- Turn the variable 'gr' in this data-frame in to an 'ord' factor.
- Assign the variable 'am', the value 'at' in case its value is one, and 'mn' in case value is zero.
- Convert the new variable 'am' into a factor.

When you run the code, you'll have the following outcome:

```
> str(r)
'data.frame': 30 obs. of 5 variables:
$ cyl   : num  5  7 4   7   9 ...
$ mpg  : num  15 18 22 20 18 ...
$ hp    : num  18 19 20 22 21 ...
$ gr    : ord.factor w/ 4 levels "4"<"5"<"6": 3 3 3 2 2 ...
$ am   : Factor w/ 2 levels "at", "mn": 3 3 3 1 1 ...
```

These were some of the ways to summarize your data.

****

In this chapter, we discussed the various ways to efficiently manipulate your data. We discussed how to get your data in & out of R, how to effectively manipulate and process your data, and how to summarize your data.

.

In the next chapter, we'll talk about how to work with Graphics.

Chapter Seven: How to work with Graphics

In this chapter, we'll talk about how to work with Graphics. We'll discuss how to use base graphics, and how to create Facetted Graphics using Lattice.

How to use base graphics

R comes with extremely potent graphics potential, which can immensely assist you to envision your data. And, it's all possible due to the base graphics.

Ways to create diverse forms of Plots:

In R, to build a plot, you need to utilize the base graphics function known as plot( ). Such a potent function has numerous preferences and arguments, to manage almost everything.

To embark with plot, you have to lay down data to utilize, first-of-all. Here, we'll utilize an in-built data-set called 'islands', which consists of the data regarding the continents, and certain big islands of our Planet. **Note:** The in-built data-sets in R are recognized in the similar way as functions are recognized. To know more about it just type: **?islands**.

The initial step is to build a subset of the 5 biggest islands in the data-set. The below mentioned code classifies (sorts) the islands in descending order, and after that, utilizes the **head( )** function to extract only the initial 5 constituents:

> big.isl <- head(sort(islands, descending = TRUE), 5)

You can even generate a plot with helpful titles as well as labels by typing the following:

> plot(big.isl, main= "Continents & Islands",

+ ylab= "Area Sq. Miles")

> text(big.isl, labels=names(big.isl), adj=c(0.5, 1))

The 1st code line constructs a basic plot utilizing the **plot( )** function, and inserts the main title as well as the y-axis (label). The 2nd code line inserts text labels utilizing the **text( )** function. You can see the result in the following figure:

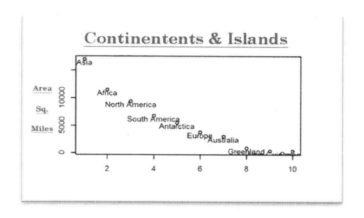

Ways to insert points to the plot:

Here, we'll utilize the in-built data-set called 'faithful'. It's a data-frame containing the information about eruptions. Now, try **plot( )** with it:

> **plot(faithful)**

The following figure displays the plot.

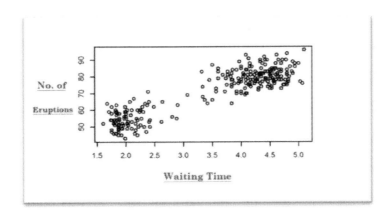

As 'faithful' is a data-frame with 2 columns, the code creates a scatter-plot with the no. of eruptions (1st column) on the y-axis, and the waiting-time (2nd column) on the x-axis.

How to add points to the plot

You need to utilize the **points( )** function to achieve this. You can check on the 'faithful' plot that there exist 2 groups. One group has smaller eruptions and their waiting-time lasts under 3.5 minutes. Now, construct a subset of 'faithful' consisting of eruptions lesser than 3.5 minutes:

> **sh.erupt <- with(faithful, faithful[No. of eruptions < 3.5,])**

Then, utilize the **points( )** function to insert all such points in green to the plot:

> **plot(faithful)**

> **points(sh.erupt, col= "green", pch=21)**

Here, the argument 'col' is utilized to alter the point's color, and the argument 'pch' is utilized to alter the 'plotting character'. The following figure displays the output:

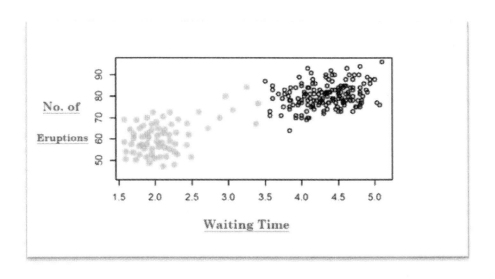

Altering the shape of the points:

Following are ways to utilize the argument 'pch' to alter the shape of the points:

- **19:** For 'Solid-Circle'
- **20:** For 'Bullet'
- **21:** For 'Filled-Circle'
- **22:** For 'Filled-Square'
- **23:** For 'Filled-Diamond'
- **24:** For 'Filled-Triangle'(Pointing upwards)
- **25:** For 'Filled-Triangle' (Pointing downwards)

These were some of the ways to use the base graphics. Next, we'll talk about how to create Facetted Graphics using Lattice.

How to create Facetted Graphics using Lattice

Constructing data subsets as well as plotting all the subsets, permits you to observe any patterns among the diverse subsets. For instance, a general manager might wish to check specific details for various areas in a graphical form, or an ecologist might wish to examine diverse species of caterpillars, and evaluate it on a plot.

Now, a solo graphic which presents such type of concurrent observations of diverse pieces via the data is known as a faceted graphic. R comes with a unique package known as lattice which lets you to effortlessly generate such type of graphic.

How to create a lattice plot

In order to know more about lattice graphics, we'll again consider the example of the in-built data-set 'mtcars'. **Note:** You can access all the in-built data-sets of R just by typing (?) symbol followed by the data-set name, for instance, **?mtcars**:

To get the details of 'mtcars', just type the following:

> str(mtcars)

'data.frame': 30 obs. of 11 variables:

$ cyl   : num 5 5 3 5 7 5 7 5 3 3 ...

$ mpg : num 18 19 21 22 19 20 16.3 21.4 20.8 18.2 ...

$ hp   : num 120 100 94 115 150 185 258 78 97 148 ...

$ disp : num 170 140 118 356 260 ...

$ wt   : num 2.72 2.58 2.12 3.11 3.64 ...

$ drat : num 2.9 2.9 3.70 3.88 3.75 2.46 3.31 3.49 3.72 3.42 ...

$ vs   : num 1 1 0 0 1 0 1 0 0 1 ...

$ qsec : num 14.5 16 19.6 18.4 15 ...

$ gear : num 3 3 3 4 4 4 4 3 3 3 ...

$ am   : num 0 0 0 1 1 1 1 0 0 ...

$ carb : num 3 5 2 2 1 2 4 1 1 4 ...

Let's assume you wish to know the connection between gear and carburetor. The 'mtcars' data-set possess two constituents related to this information:

- **carb**
- **gear**

We'll create the scatter-plot of 'carb' against 'gear' in the following section.

How to load the lattice package

You need to inform R that you wish to utilize the 'lattice' package, and you perform this by utilizing the **library( )** function. Bear in mind that you have to carry out this at the beginning of every R session, where you wish to utilize lattice:

> **library("lattice")**

Ways to create a lattice scatter-plot:

The lattice package comes with various functions to build diverse forms of plot. For instance, to generate a scatter-plot, you need to utilize the **xyplot( )** function. Remember that it's relatively different from the base graphics. In the base graphics case, the **plot( )** function generates a range of diverse forms of plot.

Now, in order to create a lattice scatter-plot, you have to state minimum of 2 arguments:

- **Formula:** It's usually like this: (b ~ a | c). This suggests generating a plot of b against a, conditional on c. It also means to generate a plot for each exclusive value of c. Every variable defined in the formula needs to be a column in the data-frame which you state in the formula.
- **Data:** It means a data-frame which consists of the entire columns which you state in the formula. Here, the data-set is 'mtcars'.

Following is the example:

> xyplot(carb ~ gear | factor(cyl), data=mtcars)

Here, the variables 'carb', 'gear', and 'cyl' are columns in 'mtcars' data-set. Your code will generate a graphic just like the following figure.

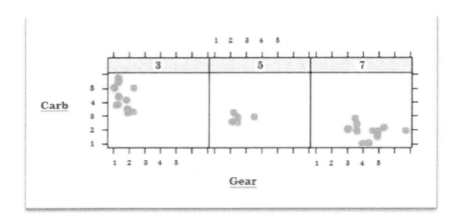

As each of the cars in the 'mtcars' data-set possess either 3, or 5, or 7 cylinders, the figure has 3 panels.

These were some of the ways to work with Graphics.

****

In this chapter, we discussed how to work with Graphics. We also talked about how to use base graphics, and how to create Facetted Graphics using Lattice.

In the next chapter, there are various exercises for you to practice.

Chapter Eight: Important exercises for practice

Following are some important exercises for you to practice:

Exercise No. 1:

- Utilizing the function **log10( )**, compute the log to the base 10 of a1 (object).
- Utilizing the function **sqrt( )**, compute the sq. root of a2 (object).
- Compute the sq. root of a2 (object) by raising it to the 0.5 (power).
- Add a1 and a2 by utilizing the function **sum( )**.
- Utilize the function **mean( )** to compute the arithmetic average of a1 and a2.
- Make an object by the name a4 that is equal to 68.7842
- Utilize the function **round( )** to round a4 to 0 (zero) decimal places.

Exercise No. 2:

- Remove the objects a1, a2, a3 and a4 which you created in the preceding exercise utilizing the **rm( )** function.
- Build a vector by the name "a1" containing the digits 11, 13, 15 and 17.
- Build a vector by the name "a2" containing the digits 12, 14, 16 and 18.
- Subtract a1 from a2.
- Build a new vector by the name "a3" by multiplying vector a1 and a2.
- Build a new vector by the name "a4" by calculating the sq. root of every element of a3.
- Utilize the **mean( )** function to compute the arithmetic average of all the digits in a4.
- Utilize the **median( )** function to compute the median of the digits in a3.

Exercise No.3:

- Utilize the function **rm( )** to remove the objects a1, a2, a3, a4.
- Build a new vector by the name "M1" containing the digits 11, 13, 15, 17, 19, 21.
- Build a matrix by the name "Z1" utilizing the function: Z1<-matrix(M1, nrows=3).
- Build a matrix by the name "Z2" similarly; however, include an additional argument 'byrow=TRUE'.
- Evaluate both of the matrices and observe how the data in vector M1 are utilized to fill up the Z1 & Z2 matrices.

Exercise No. 4:

Here, the vectors a1, a2, a3 and a4 are actually the ones which we created in exercise no. 2:

- Utilize a subscript to search the value of the 4th digit in a1.
- Utilize a subscript to search the value of the digits in a2 which aren't in the 4th position.
- Add the 2nd number in a3 to the 3rd number in a4.
- Build a new vector by the name "Jk" containing the numbers 2 and 6.
- Utilize subscripts and the vector "Jk", to build a new vector a5, which contains the sums of the 2nd and the 3rd numbers of a3 and a4.
- Compute the sum of entire numbers in a2 which are less than 18.
- Compute the mean of entire numbers in a1 which are greater than 11.

Exercise No. 5:

Here, we'll utilize the objects which we created in exercises no. 3:

- Multiply the 3rd value in the 1st row of Z1 by the 2nd value in the 3rd row of Z2.
- Build a new vector by the name "M2" that contains the following: the numbers in the 2nd row of Z1 added with the numbers in the 1st row of Z2.
- Build a new vector by the name "M3" that contains the following: the numbers in the 1st row of Z1 multiplied by the numbers in the 3rd column of Z2.
- Build a new matrix by the name "Z3" that contains the following: the 1st row of Z2 as the 1st column and then the 1st row of Z1 as the 2nd column.

These were some of the exercises for you to practice. You can find more exercises if you search on the net.

*****

The next section is a quick recap of the topics which we've covered in this guide.

Here is a quick recap of what we covered, in case you need a refresher on a certain step:

1. You now have an understanding of what exactly R Programming is, and the benefits of using R language
2. You learned how to install R and R Studio, the right code editors to begin coding R Programming, working with your code editors, the initial R session, how to source a script, and ways to navigate the workspace.
3. You learned the fundamentals of R Syntax, how to effectively use function & arguments, how to make your code plain & readable, and how to broaden R programming with user packages.
4. You learned the various ways of getting started working in R. We covered diverse topics such as fundamentals of arithmetic, how to organize data in Vectors, how to work with logical vectors, manipulating text, vector & matrix, data frames, and creation of lists.
5. You learned how to effectively Code in R. We discussed how to efficiently automate your work by utilizing functions, how to utilize arguments the smart way, how to control the Logical Flow, how to loop through different values, and how to effectively debug your Code.
6. You learned the various ways to efficiently manipulate your data. We discussed how to get your data in & out of R, how to effectively manipulate and process your data, and how to summarize your data.
7. You learned how to work with Graphics. We also discussed how to use base graphics, and how to create Facetted Graphics using Lattice.

Final Words

R has progressively gained immense recognition, as it is entirely open source and exceptionally vibrant with fresh developments. These days, it is considered imperative in various technical, or other logical streams, to possess a better knowledge of R.

This book has genuinely touched on, as well as explained, various vital topics related to the fundamentals of R. We're pretty sure that with the help of this book you can craft an incredibly firm base, and expand yourself to the numerous other applications which R has to offer.

And this brings our book to an end! We sincerely believe that this book will immensely assist you to learn the fundamentals of R language, and help you to achieve all of your future R programming objectives with GREAT SUCESS!

You may also consider learning other programming languages, your knowledge of R Programming will give you a tremendous advantage if you wish to learn other languages. You can find other popular programming books by visiting our full library >> http://amzn.to/1Xxmab2

Finally, you can also send me an email if you have any questions, feedback, or just want to say hello! (I do reply!) My email address is (Felix_Alvaro@mail.com)

I thank you once again and God bless!

Before You Go, Here Are Other Books Our Readers Loved!

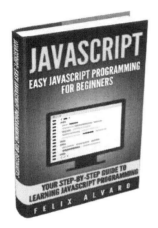

Learn Python Programming Today With This Easy, Step-By-Step Guide!

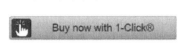

Buy now with 1-Click®

NEW

Learn Java Programming Today With This Easy, Step-By-Step Guide!

Buy now with 1-Click®

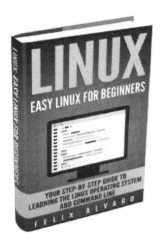

Learn The Linux Operating System and Command Line Today!

Buy now with 1-Click®

http://amzn.to/1QzQPkY

All You Need To Learn To Drive Tons Of Traffic To Your Website Today!

Buy now with 1-Click®

http://amzn.to/21HWFWb

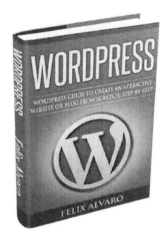

Made in the USA
San Bernardino, CA
01 September 2017